Garcia River Riffles

Porthole Views of Life

Poems

Milton Watchers

Cover Photo credit: iStockPhoto.com by license
Cover and Book design by Donna Van Sant

Garcia River Riffles
Copyright © 2015 by Milton Watchers
First Edition, November 2015

All rights reserved. No part of this book may be reproduced or transmitted in any form or by any means without written permission from the author.

ISBN: 978-0-9908075-3-7
Library of Congress Control Number: 2015953585

Designed and printed in USA by
dvs publishing
2824 Winthrop Avenue
San Ramon, CA 94583

In memory of
Harry Martin Watchers
Granddad

Contents

Miscellany

Ode to Form	3
Your Eye	4
Dance	5
Philadelphia Mint	6
Sunflower	7
Whale's Tale	8
Afghan War	9
Blackfoot Nation	10
Hope	11
Mellowing	12

Grandad's Cabin Pt. Arena

Strawberries	15
Swimming Hole	16
The Cabin (Grandad's)	17
Abalone Man	18
untitled	19
Summer	20
Logging Trail	21
Garcia River	22
Barn Cat	23
Trail	24
Trip to Cabin	25
Puddle Jumper	26

Medical

Beginner	29
Life and Death	30
Heavy with Child	31
In My Day	32
Emergency Room	33
On Call	34

Navy

First Time	37
Unknown Destination	38
Noah's Shower	39
Bangkok Hot	40
Wetting Down	41
"O K"	42
Highliner	43
Tiger/Tiger	44
Typhoon	45
Evening Shift MD	46
Boiler Room	47
Ethereal	48

Harstine Island

Dana Passage Reflections	51
Morning	52
Dana Passage	53
Harstine Beach 1	54
The Junkman	55
Harstine Beach 2	56
Wind	57
Hole in the Wall	58

Family

Mom	61
Remembering	62
Thirteen	63
Are We There Yet?	64

Sitka

Caw Caw Caw	67
Totem	68
Cold	69

About the Author   71

Miscellany

Ode to Form

                                                     Begin here?

                              I am lost

I have my margin tossed

                                         Deep in thought

          What have I wrought?

I am misplaced

                    But not erased

Will this cursed verse ever end?

                      Only when I find

My margin again!

                          February 2010

Your Eye

This is your eye

Seeing but blind

Visions of hope

Clouded by life

Sparkling nuances

Changing shapes

Gaining wisdom

Feeling hope

Losing despair

Wonderful pupil

January 2012

Dance

First seen across the floor
Eyes sparkling
Words lost
Partner evermore

He was new
Not knowing what to do
Eight strangers in a square
Waiting for a call

Music beckoning all
Partner left
Corner right
Movement a delight

Waist embraced
Weaving, swinging
Forward, backward
Hypnotic rhythm

February 2012

Philadelphia Mint

Presses noisily running, clanging

Coins everywhere

Rolling, sliding onward

Piling in buckets

I recall

Real gold and silver

Items of worth

Collectables now

That's centsable

Sunflower

Ever tracking

Morn to eve

Like a compass

To the sky

Birds delight

Squirrels revel

Tasty roasted

With sea salt

October 2012

Whale's Tale

Barnacles riding high

Grand view of sky

Slapping flapping

Downward ride

Suddenly submerged

Firmly attached

Good life on the deep

October 2012

Afghan War

Pictures on TV

Printed names only

No voice silently

From small towns

Death before life

Abandoned shell

Forgotten

Gift made

For what reason?

November 2010

Blackfoot Nation

On the high plains

Cold and bright

Into tepee

Smoky and warm

Elders at center

Curve of horseshoe

Medical volunteer

Smoked pipe

Now part of tribe

Returning gifts received

Circle now complete

November 2008

Hope

Oncology clinic 2011

Drip, drip, drip, drip drip

Quiet sunlit room

Nurses scurrying

Informal ballet

Scarves worn into battle

Quiet conversation

Others dozing, reading

Drip, drip, drip, drip

Time edging bye

Tears shed quietly

Drip, drip

Treatment done

Til next one

Port resting

2011

Mellowing

Forgive the hand sign given

Drive on beyond the horn

For you are just beginning

To accept the norm

Courtesy is lost

Amongst the traffic din

Not to respond takes courage

In the end a win

To soften rage

At any age

Makes one a sage

Free from the cage

Grandad's Cabin
Pt. Arena

Strawberries

Pt. Arena 1941

Six miles to town

Up hill and down

Dusty dirt road

Suddenly aware

Sweet aroma everywhere

Strawberry field

Small but sweet

Near a farmhouse

On the porch

Shaded from heat

Two bits a basket

Worth a repeat

January 2013

Swimming Hole

Sunlight and Heat reflect off gravel bar

Smooth pebbles burn the toes

In the shade riffles run

Filling the large dark pool

Redwood smell fills the air

Chattering chipmunks everywhere

Tadpoles in the shallows

Old steelhead deep

Worn step shoulders current

Icy clear water beckons

Cool the feet

I take the plunge

July 2012

The Cabin (Grandad's)

> Pt. Arena, near Garcia
> River @ 1940

In a clearing in the redwoods
On a quiet sunlit morning
Smell of bracken in the air
The cabin stands

Fine stucco siding
Neat corrugated roof
Redwood trim
Built with love

Filling woodbox
Lighting woodstove
Oatmeal cooking
A joy being with him

February 2012

Abalone Man

Pt. Arena, 1940

Tire iron in hand

He stood in the sand

Back to the land

Burlap bag ready

Viewing the reef

Tide running out

Looking for mollusks

Hidden away

Clasped onto rocks

Pearly inside

A tasty treat

Like buffalo

Now in retreat

February 2011

untitled

> Summer, 1940, Garcia River

On the bank of the river

In the morning dew

Abandoned orchard

Derelict Cabins in a row

Rotten wooden walk

Bunkhouse leaning

Old farmhouse blind

Acid redwood smell

Sweet fallen apples

Discarded trash

Fond memories

Fishing camp

No more

September 2010

Summer

        Garcia River, 1940

    His jeans well worn
    Shirt tail out
    Ragged and dusty
    A little forlorn

        He stood by the creek
        His feet in the water
        Feeling the current
        Cold and crisp

Cows ambled by
Time for milking
Barn cats awaiting
A squirt or two

        Milk cooling
        In the riffles
        Red evening sky
        Bats whizzing by

Milk in the creel
Up the old trail
Back to cabin
With joyful heart

    June 2010

Logging Trail

Cool and Quiet
In the shade
Redwoods tower
Softly treading

        Yellow nanna slug
        Climbs debris
        Wasps nest
        Hums actively

Out of shade
Past old deserted cabin
Lizards lollygagging
On a stump

        Down the hill
        Past Nutmeg tree
        Noisy chipmunks
        Happily sing

Part of trail
I became
There was
No time

April 2010

Garcia River

Deep water hole

In the cool shade

Surrounded with bracken

Huge sunken stumps

Tumbled old boulders

Trout close to bank

On rushing water

Bubbling gurgling

Riffles in sunlight

Over worn cobbles

Wet redwood smell

Fish in the creel

Back to the cabin

Along logging trail

May 2009

Barn Cat

Garcia River, 1941

Balmy summers' eve

Red glow in sky

Shadows in canyon

Sweet smell of hay

River rushing by

Cooling milk

In shallows

Cast bait into riffle

Hook a nice trout

Feels heavy

Barn cat heavy

Wily feline wins

June 2009

Trail

Garcia River, 1940

Leaving the cabin at sunrise

Crisp acrid smell of forest

Following logging trail to river

Dark under canopy enveloped by ferns

Enclosed by silence

Broken by river sound

Around redwood onto rocky bank

Narrow wooden bridge with riffle

below

Time to catch trout

September 2014

Trip to Cabin

Oakland to Pt Arena, 1938

Out the front door loaded for bear
'38 Ford 4-door waited there
Filled with cigar smoke
From great uncle George

Waiting for ferry
A foggy day
Smelling salt air
Wet deck chair

Off to café for chocolate
Always a treat at sea
Fog lifting slowly
Slip just ahead

Winding road to Jenner
Then over cliffs we sail
Stopping for lunch on roadside
Then finding bush

Along the coast road
Slowly until Pt. Arena
Canterbury Lodge
Finally

January 2015

Puddle Jumper

> Berkeley, 1950

She glowed and shone

A golden radiance

1933 Plymouth coupe

Lacquered deeply

Four on the floor

Bud vase by the door

Suicide exits

Wire wheels around

Bumpers '47 DeSoto

6 cylinders sound

Earned with sweat

Young man's delight

Dear uncle's labor

A gift from the heart

> October 2014

Medical

Beginner

His hand steady

Heart ready

Scalpel poised

Years of study

Culminating

Incision made

Babe in sight

Head in hand

Delivery made

Meconium blood

Mixed with water

Slippery babe

Passed off table

Closing carefully

For the first time

November 2010

Life and Death

> Large Hospital, 1992

Noisy bright lit cubicle
Monitors, IVs everywhere
Eyes closed, chest tube moving air
Sweat dampened hair

Flat line on her EEG
She was present but not there
Ultrasound Eight months along
Fetus moving for time being

Life support or death
Who arrived too soon
Decisions made
Family, doctors all agreed

Respectful quiet in OR
Child delivered noisy now
Support removed by family
She was with us for awhile

2015

Heavy with Child

> Tulare County Health
> Center, 1986

She came with a plea

Her work too heavy

Harvesting grapes

In the heat of the day

She was dressed

In worn elegance

Faintly smiling with hope

Seven months at a glance

I wrote the note

Sixty pound lugs

Were too much

To tote

<undated>

In My Day

Familiar faces

Voices raised

Hair combed over

Old wars reordered

Missing soldiers

All remembered

Problem cases

Reviewed again

We would have

Done better

Now

But count the good

We did

<undated>

Emergency Room

OB attending to E R stat

No dawdling with that

A special key for elevator

Drop seven floors

Through crowded halls

To E R automat

Doors open to chaotic din

Past lost souls cuffed to gurneys

Into room filled with staff

Patient pale and sweaty

Abrupted placenta on ultrasound

To O R stat

Live baby girl

Mom is better after blood

May 2011

On Call

Tulare District Hospital, 1987

Ring, ring, ring
Yes I am on call (sleepily)
Due last week?
Every ten minutes
Membranes ruptured?
No
Five centimeters
Fast first labor
On my way
Dive into jeans
Shirt askew
Out the door
Foggy night
Windows down
Drive by sound
Hospital glowing
Baby girl

<undated>

Navy

First Time

> Near Wake Island,
> USS Okanogan, 1960

Riding the high line from ship to ship

Wasn't like the usual zip

Anesthesia to provide

Spinal needle at my side sailor on table

Wide eyed and terrified

With reassurance

I spoke "my first spinal at sea"

Sailor replied "my first surgery!"

Appendix removed successfully

May 2015

Unknown Destination

USS Okanogan APA 220 1959

Three weeks at sea
Very thirsty
Arrived Yokosuka
Expecting liberty
Was not to be
A limo appeared
Just for me

Orders cut
Away we flew
Across Tokyo
To Camp Zama
For school

What a surprise
To learn about
Poisonous snakes
Of Indochina

October 2012

Noah's Shower

USS Okanogan APA 220 1960

Tied up on the quay
In Saigon on Mekong
Tropical hot
Everything is wet
Gecko wilted on bulkhead
Sweaty glass in hand
Lethargic in shade
River moving slowly
Mind benumbed
Everything is still
Distant rumble
Sunset glows
Breeze brings a drop or two
Sky darkens with deluge
Out of cabin naked now
Onto deck with soap and rag
Heat is broken
I am clean

October 2009

Bangkok Hot

Officers Mess Caterer

Naked in bunk

Awakened in a sweat

Pillow soaked

6am hot

Showered

Dried but wet

Tropical uniform

10am hotter

Off to buy

Pineapples for mess

Bargained in field

Too long

No shade

2pm Scorched

Five cents each

Cool deal

April 2009

Wetting Down

Upon promotion

A Naval tradition

Quenching the thirst

Of fellow officers

Blood colored sky

On the veranda

Subic Bay O Club

Where we assembled

San Miguel flowed

Like water from heaven

In sizzling weather

We were together

Excused from dinner

Under the weather

May 2009

"O K"

USS Okanogan APA 220

Steady course

Calm sea

Engines turning

Ship vibrating

Sun springs in the east

Golden turquoise sky

Rainbows in the bow wave

Porpoises slide by

Horizon bent by sky

Albatross on high

Sextant out

Shoot the sun

A true run

Quiet "Watch"

February 2009

Highliner

USS Okanogan 1959

Beautiful cruising
Three ships at dawn
Salt in air
Sea smooth as velvet

Called to the bridge
Work to be done
Surgery on ship
Just yards away

Carried in steel basket
Hung like clothesline
Pendulum swinging
Hope for true course

Colorful flying fish
Breaking bow wave
Beautiful view
Of ship astern

Clank of railing
Safely arrived
Now to surgery
Then to return

April 2010

Tiger/Tiger

USS Okanogan APA 220
Saigon 1959

Two weeks at sea

We were all dry

Tied up in Saigon

Liberty beckons

Curbside bar

Tiger beer ordered

Eagerly quaffed

One says tastes awful

Sunset reflection

Gecko in bottle

Free round for all

<undated>

Typhoon

USS Okanogan APA 220

Heaving, turning, shifting shaking

Rolling, pitching metal twisting

Plunging, rising ever forward

Engines striving groaning straining

Cold bologna sandwiches, bitter coffee

Stomachs in a knot

Life lines taut, hatches tight

Huge waves envelope the bow

Greasy, bitter salty air

Then   calm

For the old girl

May 2008

Evening Shift MD

Long Beach, CA 1960

Working in the clinic

On call for ships

Parked along the quay

Serving in the Navy

Just two more days

Called to destroyer

Emergency

Sailor hanging from a beam

Cut down

Shipmates' kiss of life

Futile

He is gone

What a waste

A part of me

June 2009

Boiler Room

USS Hornet CVA 12
Docent

No sales pitch

Nasty itch

Hot as a bitch

Steamy cauldrons

Bubbling, boiling

Water on the level

Firebox glowing

Super steam creeping

Pushing turbines

Endlessly

March 2013

Ethereal

NAS / Fallon NV

Numbers in the sky

F-15, F-16, F-18

Soaring, roaring

Almost touching climbing high

Floating like a leaf

Lethal weapons bared

No drone in the sky

Diving on humanity

Beauty and the beast

September 2011

Harstine Island

Dana Passage Reflections

Waves crashing

Tides flooding

Beach smelling

Moon reflecting

Dawn bursting

Seal fishing

Freighter passing

Tug towing

Log raft floating

Man beach combing

Agate gleaming

April 2011

Morning

Coffee cup in hand

Mount Rainier

Cross passage

O'er opposite shore

Tide ebbing

Whirling swirling

Water bright

In morning light morning addiction

What a delight

August 2010

Dana Passage

Silent ripples

Debris floats

Icy waters

High tides

Penetrating cold

Cloudy skies

Winter clings

Raven sings

February 2010

Harstine Beach 1

Cobbles gravel sand

Crushed oyster shells

Agates burning bright

Barnacles delight

Tide sliding out

Sea stars drilling

Empty clam shells

Iodine smell

Stranded jellyfish

Scurrying crablets

Circle complete

February 2010

The Junkman

For Leroy Waggoner

My friend is shrunken with age

He loses his words and is deaf

A stroke has crippled him

His house and barn are full of memories

Family wants him in a home

But he is home

His spirit is strong and feisty

He will always be my friend

October 2008

Harstine Beach 2

Cold, calm salty water

Reflecting the sky and opposite bank

Sand and barnacle clad cobbles

Old surf-worn logs and bits of flotsam

Rare agates with captured sunshine

Time to think

The noisy crow and eagle shriek

Footprints disappearing with the tide

A tug passing in the night

May 2008

Wind

Southeast gale

Gusty blustery

Whirling swirling

Bending breaking

Swaying staying

Arm in arm

Trees dance

(undated)

Hole in the Wall

Dusty dirt road narrows

Two lanes to one

Winding descent

Into canyon begun

Cool green and quiet

Sweet forest smell

Firs shading ferns

Road following creek

To tidal lagoon

Named "Hole in the Wall"

June 2013

Family

Mom

Tall, large frame, strong body

A farmer's daughter

Full of life and fun

Sharing tub with me

At three

Sitting on stoop happily

Hugged, "be a good boy"

Off to have baby

Then she was gone

<undated>

Remembering

Forgotten mornings when he walked with his mother

She was a tall rangy farmer's daughter
Sharing a bath at two
Pulling on the leash at three
I was a toddler

Then she left to have a baby
A kiss goodbye
Be a good boy
And she was gone

November 2011

Thirteen

Braces off!

Rubber taste gone

Beautiful pearlys

All in a row

Smile blinds all

Outside on Flexi

Roll down street

Hi curb

Chip front tooth

No more smile

Until it's repaired

Much later as

Cost is so dear

Ever since

Modest smile

October 2009

Are We There Yet?

Large tent, Coleman stove

Margie checks her list

Sleeping bags and food for six

Other essentials clothes and toys

Everything in its place

Station wagon ready to go

Sighs and groans with the load

Up at five and on the road

Four young children carefully placed

Greg, Beth, Ann and Carol

Beth says that's she's hungry

Reminding me to stop and feed the

Starving family

After lunch Margie's exhausted

And the children ask, are we there yet?

May 2008

Sitka

Caw Caw Caw

Sliding into bird bath

Peanut clenched in beak

Washing it then self

Darting black arrow

Raucous noisy creature

Brings a bright day

June 2012

Totem

> Totem Park, Sitka,
> Alaska

Under the bear

Beneath the raven

Wide smile

Bulging eyes

Searching for flies

Tongue alert

Bearing the burden

With guile

No hopping away

May 2011

Cold

    Crispy crunchy   cold
Hvark

    Slippery slidy   cold
Rak

    Bone aching   cold
Puc

    Erect nipple   cold
Scrat

    Icy red nose   cold
Humphic

    Car no start   cold
Whac

    Winter in Sitka   cold
Says Raven

January 2010

About the Author

Milton Watchers was born in Oakland and raised in Berkeley, California. He graduated Phi Beta Kappa from U. C. Berkeley in 1955 and from UCSF in 1958. With the rank of Lt. MC, US Navy Reserve, Dr. Watchers served from 1957 to 1962, active duty 1959-1961.

Specializing in Obstetrics & Gynecology, he worked in large urban hospitals in the San Francisco Bay Area. Now retired, in addition to many other activities, he has finally collected his poetry in one place.

Milton Watchers, MD, FACOG